"The only tired I was,
was tired of giving in."

— ROSA PARKS

ROSA PARKS

By L. S. Summer

The Child's World

GRAPHIC DESIGN
Robert E. Bonaker / Graphic Design & Consulting Co.

PROJECT COORDINATOR
James R. Rothaus / James R. Rothaus & Associates

EDITORIAL DIRECTION
Elizabeth Sirimarco Budd

COVER PHOTO
Portrait of Rosa Parks / Schomburg Center for Research in Black Culture

Library of Congress Cataloging-in-Publication Data
Summer, L. S., 1959-
Rosa Parks / by L. S. Summer
p. cm.
Summary: Examines the life and accomplishments
of Rosa Parks, as well as her impact on
the civil rights movement.
ISBN 1-56766-622-1 (library : reinforced : alk. paper)

1. Parks, Rosa, 1913- — Juvenile literature. 2 Afro-American
women — Alabama — Montgomery — Biography — Juvenile
literature. 3. Afro-Americans — Alabama — Montgomery —
Biography — Juvenile literature. 4. Civil rights workers —
Alabama — Montgomery — Biography — Juvenile literature.
5. Afro-Americans — Civil rights — Alabama —
Montgomery — Juvenile literature. 6. Segregation in
transportation — Alabama — Montgomery — History —
20th century — Juvenile literature. 7. Montgomery (Ala.)
— Race relations — Juvenile literature. 8. Montgomery
(Ala.) — Biography — Juvenile literature.
[1. Parks, Rosa, 1913-. 2. Civil rights workers. 3. Afro-
Americans — Biography. 4. Women — Biography] I. Title

F334.M753P388 1999
323'.092 — dc21   99-19251
[B]   CIP

Contents

December 1, 1955

On December 1, 1955, an *African American* named Rosa Parks rode a bus in Montgomery, Alabama. That day, a white man asked for her seat. Rosa refused to give it up. An Alabama law said blacks had to give up their seats to whites. Rosa was arrested for breaking that law.

Many people have said that Mrs. Parks was simply too tired to get up. This is not true. On that day, she made an important choice. She decided not to let white people treat her poorly. Her choice helped other blacks see that they could refuse to accept unfair rules. They could do something when people treated them poorly.

African American *slaves* were freed in the United States after the *American Civil War.* Even then, most blacks did not have equal rights. They usually lived in the worst parts of town. Their children received little or no education. Life was especially difficult for blacks in the South. Many white southerners felt *prejudice* toward blacks. They created laws to keep blacks and whites apart. This was a system known as *segregation.*

Blacks and whites were separated in any place where they could meet each other. Black children could not attend the same schools as white children. Black families could not eat in white restaurants. They could not use white swimming pools. They could not see movies at white theaters. Public restrooms and drinking fountains had signs that read "Whites Only" and "Colored Only." In Montgomery, blacks and whites couldn't even play cards, checkers, or dominoes together. There were laws against it.

Public buses also had segregation rules. In the 1920s, blacks in parts of the South could not ride inside a bus. Instead, they had to ride on top with the luggage. By the 1950s, blacks could ride inside, but they had to sit in certain seats.

Express Newspapers/Archive Photos

ALMOST EVERY PUBLIC PLACE IN THE SOUTH HAD SEGREGATION RULES. ROSA PARKS BELIEVED THAT THE LAWS WERE MEANT TO MAKE BLACK PEOPLE FEEL INFERIOR.

CORBIS-Bettmann

UNTIL THE **1960s**, BUSES IN THE SOUTHERN UNITED STATES HAD STRICT RULES. THESE LAWS WERE MEANT TO KEEP BLACKS AND WHITES APART.

There were 36 seats on each bus operated by Montgomery City Lines, Inc. The 10 seats in the front were reserved for whites only. Even if there were no whites on the bus, blacks could not sit in the front seats. Instead, they had to sit in the last 10 seats of the bus. The bus drivers could choose which passengers sat in the 16 seats in the middle. Blacks could take the seats only if no whites wanted them.

The bus drivers were required by law to enforce segregated seating. They carried weapons to make sure people did as they were told. They also had the help of police when they needed it. Almost no one dared to challenge the segregation rules. If they did, they might end up in jail.

On the day of her arrest, Rosa sat down in one of the middle seats. There were three other black people sitting in the same row with her. A white man boarded the bus. The driver told all four blacks to stand up so that one white man could sit down. The other three seats had to remain empty. Blacks and whites could not sit together in the same row.

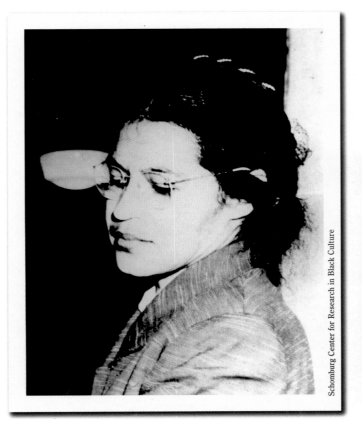

Schomburg Center for Research in Black Culture

ROSA PARKS WAS ARRESTED FOR REFUSING TO GIVE UP HER SEAT TO A WHITE MAN. SHE KNEW THE LOCAL SEGREGATION LAWS, BUT SHE WAS TIRED OF LETTING PEOPLE TREAT HER POORLY. SHE DECIDED IT WAS TIME TO STAND UP FOR HERSELF.

The three other blacks got up. Mrs. Parks stayed in her seat. Why should three seats remain empty while black people stood? She knew it was one way that whites tried to make blacks feel inferior. Rosa was tired of it. She was not going to get up.

The bus driver asked her again to give up her seat. Mrs. Parks simply said, "No." The driver said he was going to have her arrested, and he called the police.

Two policemen came to arrest Mrs. Parks. They took her to jail. She cooperated and stayed calm throughout the humiliating process. She asked a policeman why they treated black people so badly. He said he didn't know, but the law was the law. Rosa Parks was taken to the Montgomery jail for violating the laws of segregation.

CORBIS-Bettmann

AFRICAN AMERICANS KNEW THAT THE SEGREGATION RULES ON THE CITY BUSES WERE UNFAIR. STILL, THE BUSES PROVIDED THEIR TRANSPORTATION TO AND FROM WORK. MOST PEOPLE WERE AFRAID TO FIGHT BACK.

CORBIS-Bettmann

THE ARREST OF ROSA PARKS LED MANY AFRICAN AMERICANS TO
QUESTION THE WAY WHITE PEOPLE TREATED THEM. SOON, MANY
BLACKS DECIDED TO FIGHT AGAINST SEGREGATION.

Like most African Americans at the time, Rosa's grandparents had once been slaves. They were freed after the Civil War.

Growing Up

Rosa Louise McCauley was born on February 4, 1913. She was named after her grandmother, Rose Percival. Rose was a former slave. She was just five years old when the Civil War ended. For a while, the Percival family stayed on the farm where they had worked as slaves. They had never known any other way of living.

The Percivals later bought 12 acres of land in Pine Level, Alabama. They wanted to start their own farm. Grandmother Rose married a man named Sylvester Edwards. He also had been a slave. His owner had treated him very badly. He often beat Sylvester and rarely gave him food to eat. Sylvester learned to hate the way whites treated African Americans.

Sylvester and Rose had three daughters. Sylvester taught them to stand up for themselves. He believed it was wrong for whites to treat blacks unfairly. He also believed it was wrong for blacks to *tolerate* such treatment.

Sylvester also knew the importance of a good education. At the time, most girls in the South only finished the sixth-grade. This was true for both whites and blacks. Sylvester wanted more for his children. His daughter Leona graduated from high school. Then she went to college to become a teacher.

Leona taught at the town's only school for black children. Blacks had to build their own schools. They also had to take care of them. The older students chopped wood for the stoves to keep the building warm. All the students helped keep the classroom clean. White schools were built and cared for with tax money that was collected from both blacks and whites.

Leona married a man named James McCauley in 1912. James was a carpenter. He was well known in Alabama as a talented woodworker. He traveled all around the state building houses. Leona and James had two children, Rosa and her younger brother Sylvester. They named them after Leona's parents.

Leona and James could not agree about their plans for the future. Leona wanted James to get a job teaching carpentry. James wanted to keep doing construction work. He could make more money that way. He finally left his family to work in the North.

Rosa did not see her father again until she was an adult. Leona and her two children moved back to her family's farm in Pine Level. The only teaching job she could find was in another town. Leona worked there during the week and went home for the weekends.

Rosa spent a lot of time with her grandparents. She admired Grandma Rose's kindness and her faith in God. She also respected Grandfather Sylvester's strong beliefs. He believed that all people deserved fair treatment, no matter what color their skin was. These values remained important to Rosa as she grew up.

Rosa was also taught to treasure reading and education. Her mother taught her to read when she was just three years old. Rosa loved books and enjoyed going to school.

Archive Photos

A YOUNG BLACK GIRL LEAVES A SEGREGATED
RESTAURANT THROUGH A DOOR MARKED
"FOR COLORED." CHILDREN LIKE ROSA
WHO GREW UP IN THE SOUTH KNEW ALL
ABOUT THE SEGREGATION LAWS. THEY WERE
CAREFUL TO OBEY THEM.

CORBIS

WHEN ROSA WAS YOUNG, IT WAS DIFFICULT FOR BLACK CHILDREN TO GET AN EDUCATION. THEY COULD NOT ATTEND WHITE SCHOOLS. MANY HAD TO TRAVEL LONG DISTANCES TO ATTEND SPECIAL SCHOOLS FOR BLACKS.

Rosa went to the same school that her mother had attended as a child. It was an all-black elementary school with about 60 students. Rosa spent only five months a year in class. The school was closed during harvest time. During the harvest, black children had to help pick cotton. White children did not have to work in the fields. They went to school for nine months of the year.

Rosa was an excellent student. A teacher's college in Montgomery operated a school for black children. At this school, the children could study for nine months. Rosa's family decided to send her there.

When Rosa was 11 years old, she changed schools again. She went to a private school called the Montgomery Industrial School. A white woman from the North named Alice White started the school for black girls. She believed the young women deserved the chance to learn.

The teachers at the Montgomery Industrial School taught their students to have dignity and self-respect. They encouraged them to set goals. They inspired their students to believe in themselves. Rosa loved the school. She was an excellent student. To earn money for *tuition,* she helped clean the classrooms.

Unfortunately, most white people in the South did not want to help blacks. Some people in Montgomery disliked Miss White's school. They did not believe that black children should have the same opportunities as whites. The school was burned down twice. It was finally forced to close before Rosa could finish high school.

Rosa did not give up. She finished the 10th grade, but then both her grandmother and her mother became ill. She returned to Pine Level to care for them.

When Rosa was 16 years old, her grandmother died. Her mother's health had improved, but Rosa decided to stay in Pine Level. The family needed her to manage the farm.

Soon, Rosa met a young man named Raymond Parks. Raymond shared many of Rosa's values. He did not believe in letting whites treat him unfairly. Rosa admired his strong character.

Raymond and Rosa had similar experiences growing up. Raymond's father was also in the building trade and left his family when Raymond was young. Raymond could not attend the local school because he was black. There were no black schools nearby, so his mother taught him the basics at home. Later his mother became ill. Raymond cared for her until she died.

Raymond and Rosa fell in love. They were married in her mother's home in Pine Level on December 18, 1932. The young couple decided to move to Montgomery. Raymond encouraged Rosa to finish high school. In 1933, she received her diploma. She was 20 years old.

CORBIS-Bettmann

MOST AFRICAN AMERICAN FARMERS COULD NOT AFFORD TO BUY LAND. INSTEAD, THEY WORKED FOR WHITE PEOPLE. THEY OFTEN RECEIVED LITTLE PAY AND WORKED VERY LONG HOURS.

Some high schools were available for black students. Rosa attended a high school created especially for black girls until the 10th grade. Then she had to help her family run the farm.

CORBIS

WHEN ROSA AND RAYMOND MOVED TO
MONTGOMERY, THEY DISCOVERED AN ORGANIZATION
CALLED THE NATIONAL ASSOCIATION FOR THE
ADVANCEMENT OF COLORED PEOPLE (NAACP).

Standing Up for Justice

The U.S. Constitution guarantees important rights to all Americans. U.S. citizens have the right to vote, for example. They also have the right to an education. These are called *civil rights*. Unfortunately, black people have not always had these rights. Rosa and Raymond knew this from their own experiences.

In Montgomery, Rosa and Raymond learned about the National Association for the Advancement of Colored People (NAACP). The NAACP worked to help black people gain their civil rights. In 1943, Rosa joined the Montgomery *chapter* of the NAACP. She was elected its secretary and assisted the chapter's president, Mr. E.D. Nixon. Rosa and Raymond devoted much of their time and energy to the organization. One cause they felt strongly about was the right to vote.

WHITE PEOPLE OFTEN THREATENED BLACKS NOT TO VOTE IN ELECTIONS. STILL, MANY BLACK CITIZENS REFUSED TO GIVE IN. THEY KNEW THEY HAD A RIGHT TO CAST THEIR BALLOTS.

CORBIS-Bettmann

Like other U.S. citizens, all blacks had the right to vote. No one could vote if they did not register with the government first, however. Unfortunately, whites in the South tried to keep blacks from registering. Sometimes they threatened blacks who tried to register. Other times, they simply turned them away.

Rosa tried to register three times before she was finally successful. One day in 1943, Rosa had tried to register to vote and was turned away. It was a frustrating experience. The day continued to get worse. On her way home, she had her first difficulty with the Montgomery bus company.

On every Montgomery bus, blacks had to enter through the back door. The fare box was in the front, however. Blacks had to get on the bus through the front door and pay their fare. Then they had to get off the bus, walk to the back door, and board the bus again. Sometimes bus drivers would pull away before black passengers reached the back door — even after they had paid their fare.

That day, Rosa boarded the bus at the front door and paid her fare. The bus was very crowded. Blacks who were forced to stand blocked the rear doorway. Rosa could not see a good reason to get off the bus, walk to the back door, and then struggle to push her way through the entry. Instead, she turned down the aisle and walked directly to the back of the bus.

The bus driver ordered her to exit and enter again through the back door. Rosa patiently explained that she was already on the bus. She saw no need to get off. The driver ordered her to do as he said or get off the bus altogether. Rosa did not move.

The driver rose from his seat and walked back to where Rosa stood. He threatened her and angrily pulled on her coat sleeve. Rosa knew that he had a gun. She decided to get off the bus and wait for the next one.

CORBIS-Bettmann

BLACK CITIZENS IN THE SOUTH WAITED IN LONG LINES TO CAST THEIR BALLOTS. THEY WERE PROUD TO HAVE THE RIGHT TO VOTE.

A reporter interviews Rosa before her trial. Mr. Nixon (second from left) of the NAACP hoped that Rosa's trial could be used to fight segregation.

For the next 10 years, Rosa watched for the same driver. She never got on the bus when he was driving. On December 1, 1955, Rosa was lost in her thoughts as she boarded the bus. She was thinking about a NAACP conference that she was organizing. She boarded the bus without looking at the driver. It was the same man who threatened her more than 10 years earlier! When Rosa refused to give up her seat, he had her arrested.

At least three other blacks had been arrested on Montgomery buses. Many more were threatened or shamed. The bus company employed only white drivers. Many of the drivers were unkind or even cruel. Something had to change.

No one realized that Rosa Parks' arrest would trigger that change. Two important things happened after Rosa's arrest. First, Rosa and the NAACP would get the chance to take her case to the nation's most important court. A year earlier, the Supreme Court had decided that it was illegal to have segregated schools. NAACP leaders planned to take Rosa's case before the Supreme Court as well. They hoped the court would decide that bus segregation was also wrong.

On December 5, Rosa Parks was found guilty. She was fined $10, plus $4 in court costs. This was the result Mr. Nixon and the NAACP wanted. If an American is found guilty, he or she can ask a more important court to reconsider the *verdict*. This process is called an *appeal*. Now Rosa and the NAACP could take her case to a higher court.

A second important result of the arrest was the Montgomery Bus *Boycott*. Before Rosa's trial, a group called the Women's Political Council sprang into action. They passed out 35,000 flyers asking blacks to stay off the buses on the day of the trial — even if they had to miss a day of school or work. Word spread quickly. Soon, nearly every African American in Montgomery knew about the boycott.

Not one African American rode the bus in Montgomery that day. Some people walked to wherever they needed to go. Others took taxis with African American drivers who charged only the price of a bus ride. Blacks who owned cars shuttled others back and forth all day long. People rode their bikes or walked to their destinations.

REVEREND RALPH ABERNATHY MADE A SPEECH TO ENCOURAGE MONTGOMERY'S BLACK CITIZENS TO BOYCOTT THE BUS COMPANY.

Black pastors played an important role in the bus boycott. They encouraged the members of their churches to support it. Religion was an important part of African Americans' lives. Since the days of slavery, churches were one of the few places blacks could meet freely to discuss their concerns.

After Rosa's trial was over, Montgomery's black leaders held a meeting. They wanted to see if the community should continue the boycott. Every seat was filled. Hundreds of people stood outside. A local pastor named Reverend Ralph Abernathy made a speech. So did Mr. Nixon. Then a young preacher was called upon. His name was Reverend Martin Luther King, Jr. Reverend King would soon be a respected leader of the *civil rights movement*.

It was time to vote on whether to continue the boycott. The crowd rose to their feet. Montgomery's black citizens all agreed: The boycott would go on until the segregation rules ended.

George Tames/New York Times Co./Archive Photos

MONTGOMERY CITIZENS GATHERED TO DISCUSS WHETHER THEY SHOULD CONTINUE TO BOYCOTT THE CITY'S BUSES. AFTER ROSA'S ARREST, THE BLACK COMMUNITY ROSE TO ACTION.

Schomburg Center for Research in Black Culture

DURING THE BUS BOYCOTT, ROSA GAVE MANY
SPEECHES. SHE ENCOURAGED OTHER BLACKS TO
HAVE COURAGE AND TO DEMAND THEIR RIGHTS.

Blacks refused to ride Montgomery buses for 381 days — more than one year. The city's white citizens tried everything they could to end the boycott. They even tried to frighten black people with threats and acts of violence. African Americans did not give in. For a year, black people with cars gave others a ride. Some rode horses to their destinations. Many people traveled on foot.

The Montgomery police made more arrests. Rosa Parks was arrested a second time, this time for participating in the boycott. Rosa, Reverend King, and other leaders gave many speeches about the boycott and the unfairness of the South's segregation laws.

On December 20, 1956, the Supreme Court made a decision about Rosa's case. They ordered Montgomery to *integrate* its public bus lines. The bus company's segregation rules were now illegal. The black citizens of Montgomery had won!

Blacks were free to sit anywhere on a bus they chose. White bus drivers could no longer use the law to treat black passengers badly. Most important, blacks learned that they had the power to change things. If African Americans united as a community, they could improve their lives — and those of blacks across the country.

A BLACK MAN PREPARES TO BOARD A SEGREGATED BUS BOUND FOR JACKSON, MISSISSIPPI. AFTER THE SUCCESS OF THE MONTGOMERY BUS BOYCOTT, OTHER BLACKS REALIZED THEY COULD DEMAND BETTER TREATMENT.

Express Photos/Archive Photos

She Hasn't Stopped Since

The Supreme Court decision against bus segregation could not be ignored. Unfortunately, Montgomery was a long way from Washington, D.C., the home of the court. Whites who believed in segregation were not ready to change.

Some white people threatened those who had been involved in the boycott. They bombed the homes of Martin Luther King, Jr. and E.D. Nixon. Rosa and Raymond received threatening phone calls. Rosa's mother now lived with the Parks. Some nights, she would talk to friends on the phone all night to keep the threatening calls from coming. The Parks family was afraid. Raymond kept a gun near him when he slept at night.

Many blacks lost their jobs during and after the boycott. Soon Rosa and Raymond were out of work as well. They decided it was time to leave Montgomery. Rosa's brother Sylvester lived in Detroit. In 1957, they moved there as well. Rosa's mother went with them.

Rosa had become well known. She traveled around the country to give speeches about her experiences. Meanwhile, Reverend King, Mr. Nixon, Reverend Abernathy, and others had formed a new organization. They called it the Southern Christian Leadership Conference (SCLC). It had chapters around the country. Rosa was very involved with the SCLC. She traveled to the South to attend its meetings.

CORBIS-Bettmann

ROSA PARKS RIDES IN THE FRONT SEAT OF A MONTGOMERY BUS.
THE SUPREME COURT OUTLAWED SEGREGATION ON THE CITY'S
BUSES IN 1956. STILL, MANY AFRICAN AMERICANS REALIZED
THAT MUCH MORE NEEDED TO BE DONE.

Archive Photos

PRESIDENT LYNDON B. JOHNSON SIGNED THE CIVIL RIGHTS ACT IN 1964. REVEREND MARTIN LUTHER KING, JR., ATTENDED THE CEREMONY.

The case of Rosa Parks and the Montgomery bus boycott helped launch the civil rights movement. Soon, there were other boycotts. African Americans marched in large groups throughout the South to demand better treatment. They organized "freedom rides" to integrate bus travel between states. In 1963, 200,000 people participated in the March on Washington, a *protest* in the nation's capital.

On May 2, 1964, President Lyndon Johnson signed the Civil Rights Act. Now the U.S. federal government would stand up for the civil rights of its black citizens. Still, the struggle was far from over. The new law could not instantly change people's beliefs or their behavior. Blacks still faced *discrimination*. Rosa Parks knew there was much more to be done. She continued to travel and speak out for equality.

Rosa was also very busy in her personal life. Both Raymond and her mother were in poor health. Rosa cared for them at home. In 1965, Mrs. Parks became an assistant to an African American congressman, John Conyers. Rosa respected Representative Conyers' views and ideas.

The 1970s brought difficult times. Rosa's husband Raymond died in 1977. Her brother Sylvester died three months later. Soon after, Rosa's mother moved to a nursing home that could take better care of her failing health. Rosa visited her three times each day. In 1978, Rosa moved her mother back home to care for her there. Her mother died the following year at age 91.

Rosa worked for Representative Conyers until she retired in 1988. Around that time, Rosa and her close friend Elaine Steele founded the Rosa and Raymond Parks Institute for Self-Development. This organization offers education and community programs to young people between the ages of 11 and 18. It also awards *scholarships* to African American students.

One program at the institute is called "Paths to Freedom." Children in the program have the chance to travel across the United States tracing the path of the *Underground Railroad*. They also visit the scenes of important events in the civil rights movement.

Rosa has received many awards and honors. Some of these include the Martin Luther King, Jr., Nonviolent Peace Prize (1980); the Eleanor Roosevelt Women of Courage Award (1984); the Presidential Medal of Freedom (1996); and the International Freedom Conductor Award (1998).

CORBIS-Bettmann

There have been other tributes to Mrs. Parks' courage as well. The city of Montgomery has named a street after her. Hundreds of other roads, schools, and parks around the country bear her name. The Smithsonian Institute in Washington, D.C., displays a statue of Mrs. Parks. The Rosa Parks Library and Museum will open in December 2000 in Montgomery. It will help people understand the events that led to the famous bus boycott.

Rosa Parks continues to work for equality and justice. She seems to touch everyone she meets, from children to senior citizens. Mrs. Parks believes that intelligence and self-respect are powerful weapons against prejudice. She is proof that the act of one person can change the world. Mrs. Parks continues to inspire people of all races to demand equality.

ROSA CONTINUED TO PROTEST AGAINST RACISM IN THE 1980s. SHE ATTENDED A DEMONSTRATION AGAINST APARTHEID IN 1984. APARTHEID WAS THE OFFICIAL SOUTH AFRICAN SYSTEM OF DISCRIMINATION AND SEGREGATION.

Schomburg Center for Research in Black Culture

In 1997, Mrs. Parks received more than 2,000 requests to give speeches or make appearances. She usually accepts about 100 requests each year.

Timeline

1913   Rosa McCauley is born in Tuskegee, Alabama, on February 4.

1918   Rosa starts school in Pine Level.

1924   Rosa attends school in Montgomery.

1929   Rosa leaves school to care for her grandmother.

1932   Rosa marries Raymond Parks.

1934   Rosa receives a high school diploma.

1943   Rosa joins the NAACP. She is elected secretary of the Montgomery chapter. A Montgomery bus driver forces Rosa off a bus because she refuses to exit and re-enter through the rear door.

1955   Rosa is arrested on December 1 for violating the segregation law.

1956   On February 21, Rosa is arrested a second time for participation in the Montgomery bus boycott. On December 20, the Supreme Court rules that Montgomery buses must be integrated.

1957   Rosa and her family move to Detroit.

1964   President Lyndon Johnson signs the Civil Rights Act on July 2.

1965   Rosa joins the staff of Representative John Conyers.

1977   Raymond Parks and Rosa's brother Sylvester die of cancer.

1979   Rosa's mother, Leona McCauley, dies at age 91.

1987   Rosa founds the Rosa and Raymond Parks Institute for Self-Development.

1988   Rosa retires from John Conyers' staff.

1992   Rosa publishes *Rosa Parks: My Story*.

1996   President Bill Clinton presents Rosa with the Presidential Medal of Freedom.

1998   Rosa receives the International Freedom Conductor Award.

1998   Ground is broken for the Rosa Louise Parks Library–Museum in Montgomery.

Glossary

African American
(AF-ri-kan uh-MAYR-ih-kan)
An African American is a black American whose ancestors came from Africa. Rosa Parks is an African American.

American Civil War
(uh-MAYR-ih-kan SIV-el WAR)
The American Civil War was fought between the North and South from 1861 through 1865. When the war ended, African American slaves were freed.

appeal
(uh-PEEL)
An appeal is when someone attempts to change a court's decision by asking a more powerful court to consider the case.

boycott
(BOY-kot)
A boycott is when a group of people stop using a certain product or service as a form of protest. The Montgomery Bus Boycott sent a message to the bus company that black citizens would not tolerate poor treatment.

chapter (CHAP-tur)
A chapter is a local branch of a larger organization. Rosa Parks was a member of the Montgomery chapter of the NAACP.

civil rights
(SIV-el RYTZ)
Civil rights are the personal freedoms that belong to all citizens of the United States. The Constitution guarantees civil rights.

civil rights movement
(SIV-el RYTZ MOOV-mint)
The civil rights movement was the name given to the struggle for equal rights for blacks in the United States during the 1950s and 1960s. Martin Luther King, Jr., was a leader of the civil rights movement.

discrimination
(dis-krim-ih-NAY-shun)
Discrimination is the unfair treatment of people simply because they are different. African Americans have suffered discrimination by whites.

integrate
(INT-uh-grayt)
If people integrate something, they allow it to be used equally by all races. In 1956, the Supreme Court ruled that the city of Montgomery must integrate its buses.

prejudice
(PREJ-uh-des)
Prejudice is a negative feeling or opinion about someone without a good reason. Black Americans have often faced prejudice from whites.

Glossary

protest
(PROH-test)
A protest is when people gather together in a group to show their objection to something. Americans of all races attended protests against the treatment of blacks.

scholarships
(SKAL-er-shipz)
Scholarships are sums of money awarded to students to help pay for their education. The Rosa and Raymond Parks Institute for Self-Development awards scholarships to African American students.

segregation
(seg-rih-GAY-shun)
Segregation is actions and laws that separate people from one another. Blacks and whites were segregated in the South for many years.

slaves
(SLAYVZ)
Slaves are people who are forced to work for others without pay. Slavery became illegal in the United States when the North won the Civil War.

tolerate
(TAWL-uh-rayt)
If someone tolerates something, they accept it even though it is wrong or unpleasant. Rosa's grandfather Sylvester believed it was wrong to tolerate poor treatment.

tuition
(tu-ISH-en)
Tuition is a fee for attending a private school. Rosa worked for the school to help pay her tuition.

Underground Railroad
(UN-der-grownd RAYL-rohd)
The Underground Railroad was a group of people who helped African Americans escape slavery. The Rosa and Raymond Parks Institute for Self-Development takes young people on a tour of important sites on the railroad.

verdict
(VUR-dikt)
A verdict is a decision made by a judge or a court during a trial. The Montgomery court's verdict in the trial of Rosa Parks was that she was guilty.

Index

For Further Information

Books

Friese, Kai Jabir. *Rosa Parks: The Movement Organizes* (History of Civil Rights series). Parsippany, NJ: Silver Burdett Press, 1990.

Parks, Rosa, with Jim Haskins. *Rosa Parks: My Story.* New York: Puffin, 1999.

Siegel, Beatrice. *The Year They Walked: Rosa Parks and the Montgomery Bus Boycott.* New York: Simon & Schuster, 1992.

Web Sites

The Montgomery Bus Boycott page:
http://socsci.colorado.edu/~jonesm/montgomery.html

The Troy State University Montgomery Rosa Parks:
Library and Museum
http://www.tsum.edu/museum/

The NAACP On-Line:
http://www.naacp.org

Black Information Network:
http://www.bin.com